YOUNG ZOOLOGIST
HONEY BEE

A FIRST FIELD GUIDE TO THE WORLD'S FAVORITE POLLINATING INSECT

NEON  SQUID

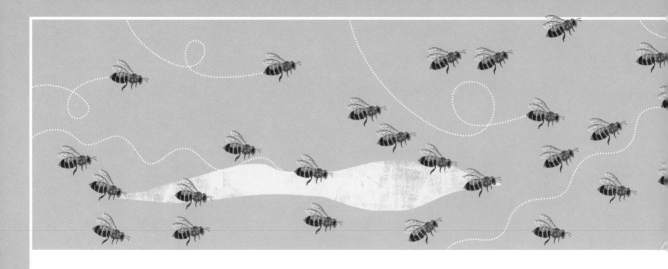

CONTENTS

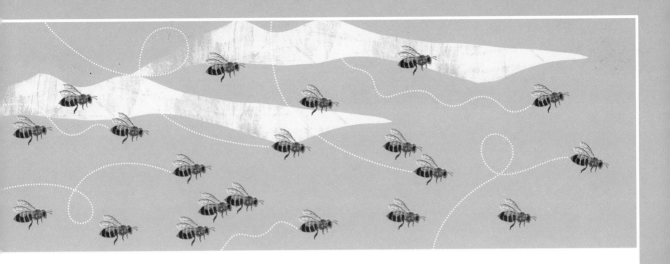

HELLO, YOUNG ZOOLOGIST!

My name is Dr. Priya Chakrabarti Basu. I am an Indian scientist who lives and works in the United States. Together we will explore the exciting and busy world of honey bees! I love honey bees because they are important pollinators and are very valuable to our ecosystems. They are also incredibly smart and have a lot to teach all of us—including how to be hard, attentive workers and how to share with others. Our journey through this book will reveal fascinating facts about the busy bees, their hives, their life cycle, and what we can do to help them. So the next time you see honey bees, you can talk to your friends about all the amazing work they do!

DR. PRIYA CHAKRABARTI BASU

FACT FILE

SCIENTIFIC NAME
Apis mellifera

CLASS
Insects

FAMILY
Bees

SIZE
There are eight species of honey bee. Giant honey bees are the largest, while red dwarf honey bees are the smallest.

Asian honey bee

Giant honey bee

European honey bee

Red dwarf honey bee

EATS
Pollen and nectar from flowers

ORDER
Hymenoptera: This is the largest insect order and includes ants, bees, wasps, and sawflies.

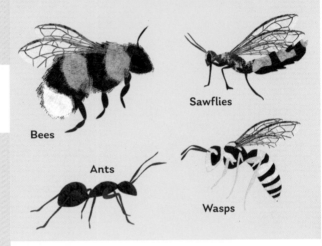

Bees

Sawflies

Ants

Wasps

LIFE SPAN
Queen: several years
Worker: one to two months
Drone: about one month

HABITAT
Worldwide, except Antarctica

BEFORE YOU GET STARTED

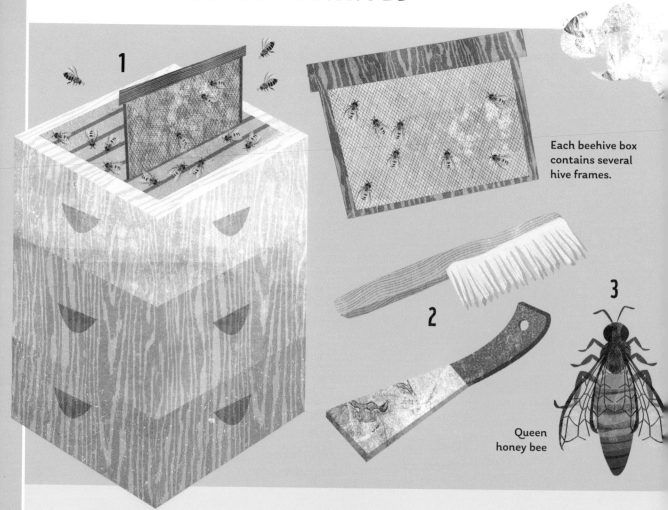

Each beehive box contains several hive frames.

Queen honey bee

1 HIVE FRAME

A hive frame is a structure inside a beehive box that holds the honeycomb and the bees inside the hive. You can remove a frame to examine the honey bees!

2 BEE BRUSH AND HIVE TOOL

A bee brush is used to gently brush honey bees away on a hive frame without harming them. A hive tool is used to remove the hive frames when inspecting the hive.

3 QUEEN AND WORKER BEES

You need a queen honey bee and worker honey bees to start a beehive. You can buy a large number of worker honey bees for your hive—they are called "package bees."

Beekeeping is a great way to watch honey bees and learn about their behavior. You can also make your own honey! As a beekeeper, you'll need important tools to help you work safely.

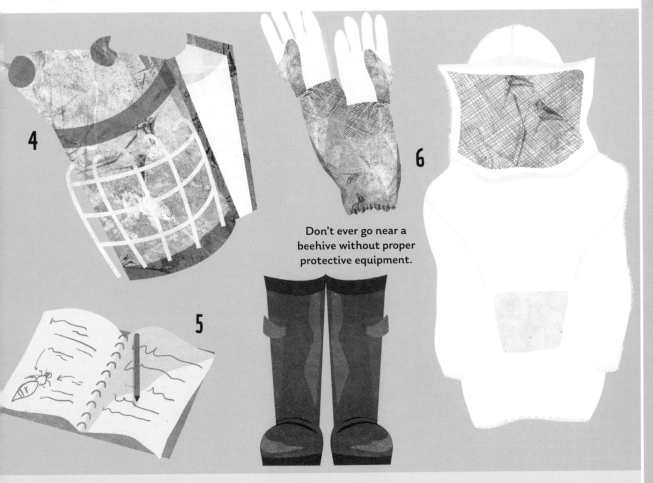

Don't ever go near a beehive without proper protective equipment.

4 SMOKER

A smoker is used to puff smoke into beehives. Smoke doesn't harm bees. Instead, it calms them and masks their sense of smell. This prevents them from stinging beekeepers.

5 NOTEBOOK AND PEN

Record what you see and take notes after a beehive inspection. You can also write down what time the honey bees are most active and what food they bring back to the hive.

6 PROTECTIVE CLOTHING

Wear a bee suit with a veil, gloves, and proper boots to prevent yourself from being stung while beekeeping. This is to protect both you and the honey bees.

MEET THE HONEY BEE

Honey bees are flying insects that can make their own honey. Their bodies have three main parts: the head, the thorax, and the abdomen. They are generally yellow and brown and have hairy bodies.

Head

Forewing

Thorax

Hind wing

Abdomen

STINGER

Located at the end of the abdomen, the stinger is a sharp point used for injecting bee venom into enemies. Bees sting when they're angry or scared.

The honey bee's stomach, or crop, holds nectar while it flies back to its colony.

HIND LEG

POLLEN BASKETS

Honey bee workers have a special area called a corbicula, or pollen basket, on each hind leg. These are used for collecting pollen from flowers.

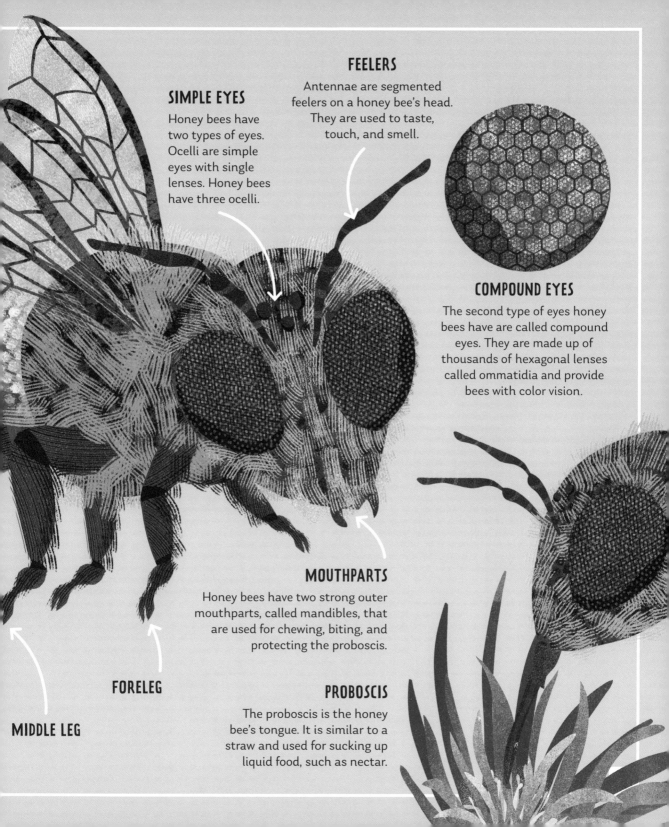

FEELERS

Antennae are segmented feelers on a honey bee's head. They are used to taste, touch, and smell.

SIMPLE EYES

Honey bees have two types of eyes. Ocelli are simple eyes with single lenses. Honey bees have three ocelli.

COMPOUND EYES

The second type of eyes honey bees have are called compound eyes. They are made up of thousands of hexagonal lenses called ommatidia and provide bees with color vision.

MOUTHPARTS

Honey bees have two strong outer mouthparts, called mandibles, that are used for chewing, biting, and protecting the proboscis.

FORELEG

MIDDLE LEG

PROBOSCIS

The proboscis is the honey bee's tongue. It is similar to a straw and used for sucking up liquid food, such as nectar.

HOME SWEET HOME

Giant honey bees in Asia like to make large, hanging nests out in the open.

NATURAL HIVES

In the wild, honey bees make their own nests where they live and raise their young. Some honey bees like open nests with plenty of light and wind. Others prefer cavity nests inside natural hollows and crevices.

Sometimes honey bees shelter in your house—inside walls or under the eaves.

Many wild honey bee colonies like to build nests inside tree hollows.

Some wild honey bee colonies can live inside rock crevices!

A family of honey bees is called a colony. A colony is made up of one queen, many workers, and some drones (see pages 12–13). A colony of honey bees can live in a natural hive they make or find, or in a human-made hive.

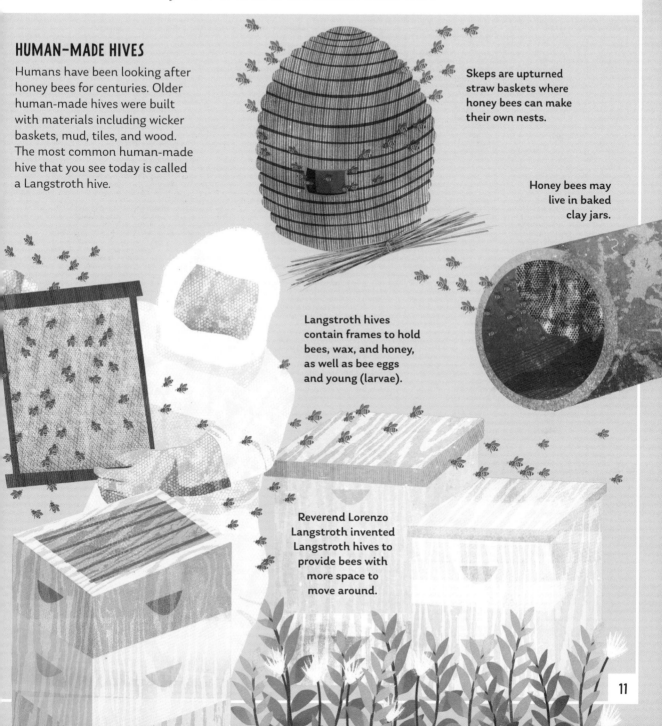

HUMAN-MADE HIVES

Humans have been looking after honey bees for centuries. Older human-made hives were built with materials including wicker baskets, mud, tiles, and wood. The most common human-made hive that you see today is called a Langstroth hive.

Skeps are upturned straw baskets where honey bees can make their own nests.

Honey bees may live in baked clay jars.

Langstroth hives contain frames to hold bees, wax, and honey, as well as bee eggs and young (larvae).

Reverend Lorenzo Langstroth invented Langstroth hives to provide bees with more space to move around.

MEMBERS OF THE COLONY

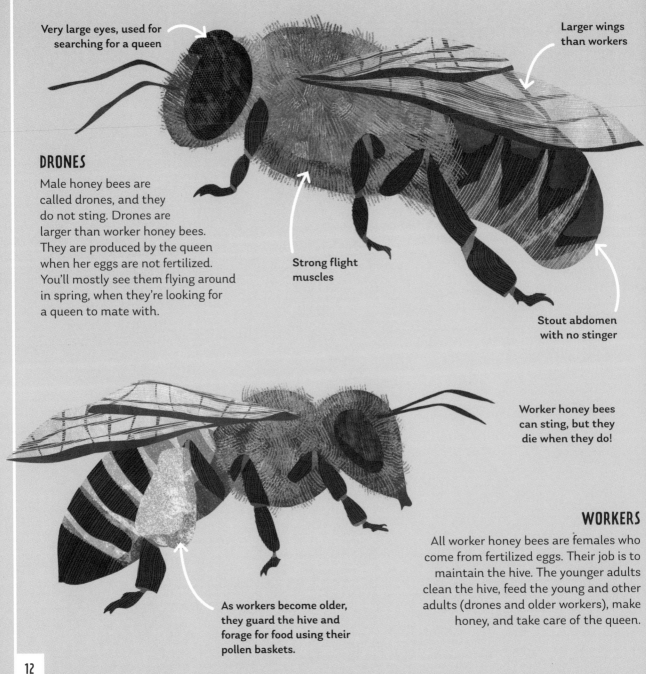

Very large eyes, used for searching for a queen

Larger wings than workers

DRONES

Male honey bees are called drones, and they do not sting. Drones are larger than worker honey bees. They are produced by the queen when her eggs are not fertilized. You'll mostly see them flying around in spring, when they're looking for a queen to mate with.

Strong flight muscles

Stout abdomen with no stinger

Worker honey bees can sting, but they die when they do!

WORKERS

All worker honey bees are females who come from fertilized eggs. Their job is to maintain the hive. The younger adults clean the hive, feed the young and other adults (drones and older workers), make honey, and take care of the queen.

As workers become older, they guard the hive and forage for food using their pollen baskets.

Honey bees are social insects, and each bee has its own job to do. There are three types (or castes) of honey bee: drones, workers, and queens. Here's how to tell the difference between them.

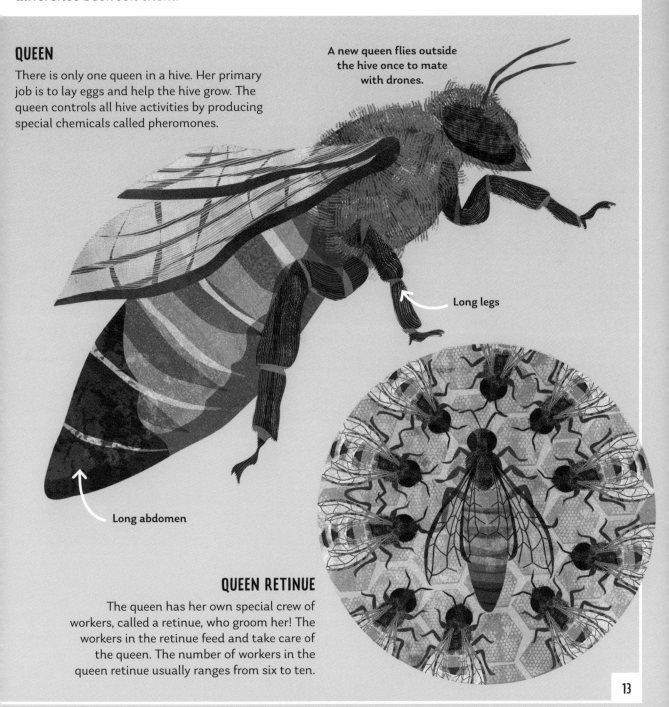

QUEEN

There is only one queen in a hive. Her primary job is to lay eggs and help the hive grow. The queen controls all hive activities by producing special chemicals called pheromones.

A new queen flies outside the hive once to mate with drones.

Long legs

Long abdomen

QUEEN RETINUE

The queen has her own special crew of workers, called a retinue, who groom her! The workers in the retinue feed and take care of the queen. The number of workers in the queen retinue usually ranges from six to ten.

BABY BEES

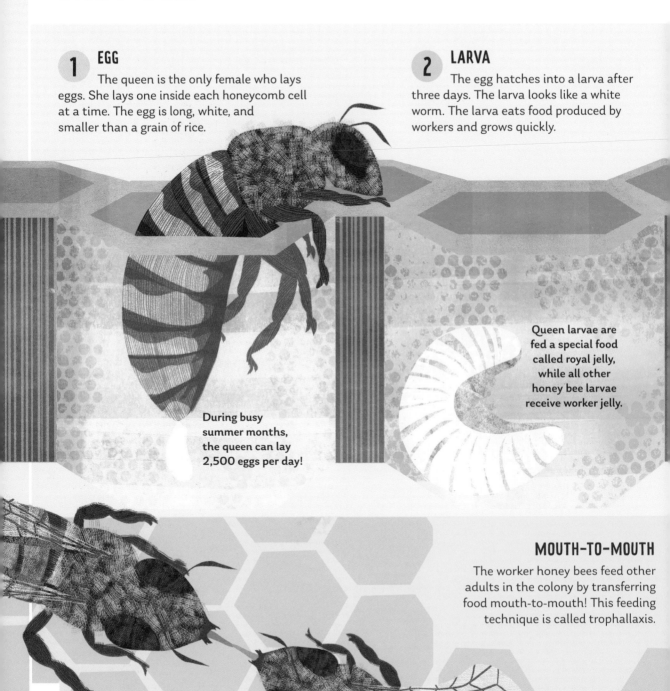

1 **EGG**

The queen is the only female who lays eggs. She lays one inside each honeycomb cell at a time. The egg is long, white, and smaller than a grain of rice.

2 **LARVA**

The egg hatches into a larva after three days. The larva looks like a white worm. The larva eats food produced by workers and grows quickly.

Queen larvae are fed a special food called royal jelly, while all other honey bee larvae receive worker jelly.

During busy summer months, the queen can lay 2,500 eggs per day!

MOUTH-TO-MOUTH

The worker honey bees feed other adults in the colony by transferring food mouth-to-mouth! This feeding technique is called trophallaxis.

A beehive is made of lots of hexagonal wax cells, which together form the honeycomb. The queen lays eggs in these hexagonal cells. There are four stages of a honey bee life cycle: egg, larva, pupa, and adult.

3 PUPA

The larva stops eating, and the honeycomb cell is capped with wax. Inside the honeycomb, the larva becomes a pupa.

4 ADULT

At the end of pupation, the honey bee has transformed and has a head, body, and wings. It is ready to emerge as an adult!

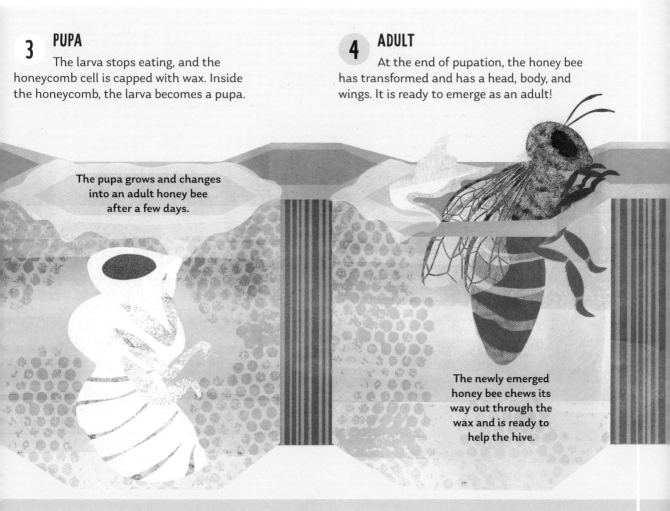

The pupa grows and changes into an adult honey bee after a few days.

The newly emerged honey bee chews its way out through the wax and is ready to help the hive.

SWARMING

Sometimes, when there are too many bees in the hive in the spring, the old queen leaves with some workers to find a new place to nest. She leaves the new queen with the other workers in the hive. This process is called swarming.

WHAT'S FOR DINNER?

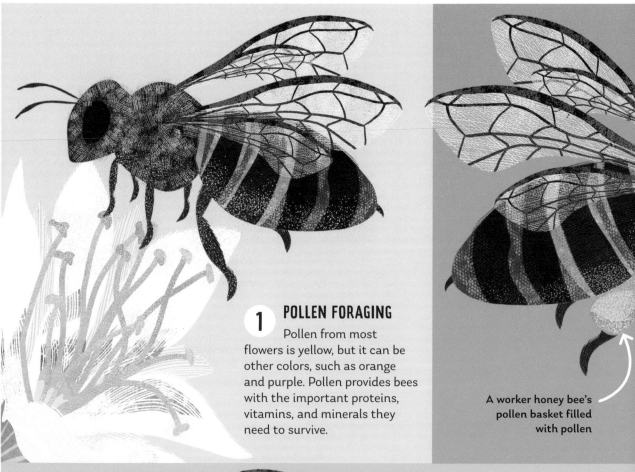

1 POLLEN FORAGING

Pollen from most flowers is yellow, but it can be other colors, such as orange and purple. Pollen provides bees with the important proteins, vitamins, and minerals they need to survive.

A worker honey bee's pollen basket filled with pollen

COLLECTING NECTAR

Worker honey bees suck nectar out of flowers using their straw-like proboscises. Nectar is a source of energy. It provides honey bees with sugars and important nutrients.

Honey bees get their food from flowers. The powder on the male parts of flowers (anthers) is called pollen. The sugary liquid at the base of the flowers is called nectar. Worker honey bees spend their days busily collecting both pollen and nectar.

2 POLLEN BASKETS

Honey bee workers collect pollen from flowers in their pollen baskets.

3 BEE BREAD

Pollen is very important for growing baby bees. Foraging honey bees bring the pollen back to the colony and store it in their honeycomb as "bee bread" to be fed to the larvae.

DIRTY WATER

Honey bees drink water, especially in the summer when it's hot. They like "dirty water" that is rich in minerals. Dirty water can be found in puddles, ponds, birdbaths, and brooks.

BUSY BEES

HIVE LIFE

Honey bees live very busy lives inside and outside their hive. Different bees perform different tasks. Together, all the bees within the hive are called a superorganism.

Honey bee foragers bring back food to the hive.

POLLINATING FLOWERS

As bees travel from flower to flower, they transfer pollen from one to another. This helps flowers produce seeds so they can grow in new places.

Honey bees collect pollen from anthers (the male parts of a flower).

When the honey bee visits another flower, she deposits pollen on the stigma (the female part of a flower).

Bees pollinate about two thirds of the plants we eat.

Honey bees play an important role in ecosystems around the world because they pollinate flowers. This helps plants produce fruit and seeds—making more plants. Many of the beautiful flowering plants around you are pollinated by honey bees!

Honey bees secrete wax from special glands to build honeycomb.

HIVE CHORES

Worker honey bees keep the hive cool in the summer by fanning their wings. In the winter they group together to stay warm. Guards protect the hive entrance.

Pollen from flowers is processed and stored as bee bread.

Worker honey bees regularly clean the hive.

Workers produce honey from nectar to store inside the hive.

Workers feed the baby bees and the queen.

DANCING BEES

ROUND DANCE

When a food source is nearby, honey bees do a "round dance" inside the hive. The dancing honey bee goes around in circles and excitedly tells other workers to look for food close to the hive.

Human vision

Bee vision

SEEING IN COLOR

Honey bees see flowers differently than humans do. They often see things that humans do not—for example, colors in the ultraviolet spectrum. Honey bees can't see the color red, but they can see flowers of all other colors, such as blue and yellow. Many flowers have unique ultraviolet patterns to attract honey bees.

Honey bees dance to communicate! Inside the hive a foraging honey bee shakes her body from side to side rapidly in certain directions. From this dance other honey bees learn where to find the best food.

WAGGLE DANCE

When the food source is far away, honey bees do a "waggle dance." This looks like a figure eight. Through this dance the forager tells her nest mates the exact direction of the food source (pollen or nectar), how far away it is, and how delicious it is!

Dr. Karl von Frisch won a Nobel Prize in 1973 for explaining the waggle dance.

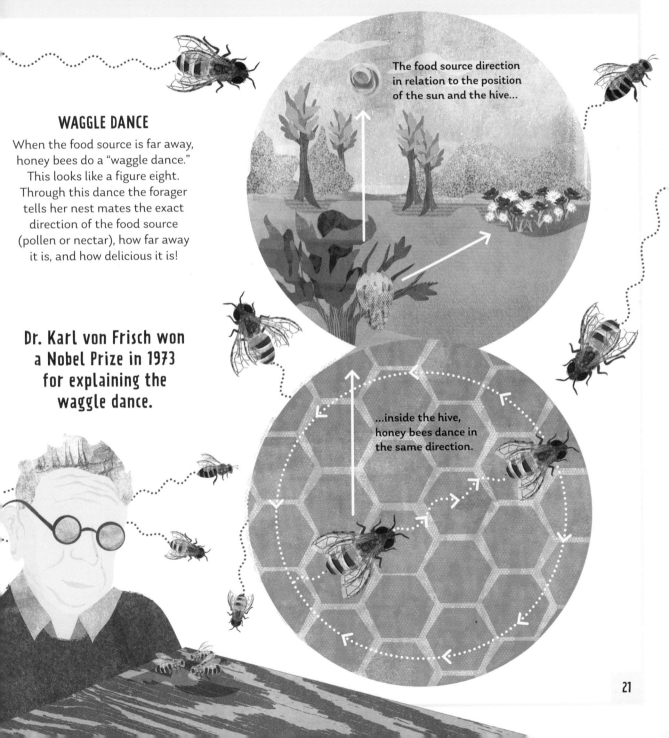

The food source direction in relation to the position of the sun and the hive...

...inside the hive, honey bees dance in the same direction.

CHANGING SEASONS

SPRING

In spring, flowers are starting to bloom and it's getting warmer. The hive awakens from its winter state. The queen is busy laying eggs and the colony is growing, while the drones are mating with new queens. The workers are busy collecting pollen and nectar, and feeding the larvae. Some of the honey bees are also ready to swarm.

SUMMER

During warm summer days, there are more flowers to collect pollen and nectar from. The honey bees are making a lot of honey inside the hive! They are storing this honey, as well as bee bread, for fall and winter. The queen continues to lay eggs.

The queen starts laying eggs.

Lots of honey!

Honey bees perform different tasks throughout the seasons, and the colony is busy for most of the year. When bees are most active outside of the hive depends a lot on the weather and the availability of flowers.

FALL

In fall, when it starts to cool down, the hive slows down. There are fewer flowers around, meaning less food for the hive. The queen stops laying eggs in late fall and early winter.

WINTER

In the cold winter months, the colony consists of a small group made up of the queen and a few workers. They keep one another warm by clustering together. The honey bees eat the honey and bee bread they stored from warmer months and wait for the next spring.

Less activity in the hive

The colony is now a small cluster.

MAKING HONEY

1 COLLECTING NECTAR

After collecting nectar from flowers, a worker honey bee stores it in its crop and flies back to the hive. One honey bee can visit 50 to 100 flowers in one trip.

Crop (stomach)

2 TRANSFERRING NECTAR

In the hive, the worker bee gives the collected nectar to a younger worker. The younger worker will process this nectar inside its stomach to make honey.

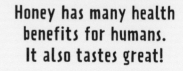

Honey has many health benefits for humans. It also tastes great!

Inside the stomach of the younger worker, a protein called invertase is added to the nectar.

Honey bees are the only type of bee that makes honey. The more flowers and worker bees there are, the more honey there is in the hive! Let's take a look at how honey bees make this super-sweet substance.

3 STORING HONEY

The invertase in the young worker's stomach makes the sugars in the nectar change. The honey bees remove water from the nectar and store it in the honeycomb.

It takes 12 honey bee workers a lifetime to make one teaspoon of honey.

4 FANNING

The worker honey bees fan the processed nectar with their wings. Fanning helps to remove more water from the processed nectar, making it thicker.

5 CAPPED WITH WAX

When the honey is ready, the honeycomb cell is capped with wax—ready for storage! Honey bees can chew open the cap and consume the honey throughout the year when nectar is no longer available.

BEEKEEPER TRICKS

SMOKING BEES

Beekeepers wear a protective bee suit, gloves, and veil so that they will not get stung. Using a smoker helps calm the bees, allowing the beekeeper to work with the hive. Smoke also masks the alarm signals of the bees.

There are about 30,000 honey bees in an average beehive. A large hive can contain more than 50,000 honey bees! A beekeeper is responsible for taking care of all of these insects. Here's how they do it.

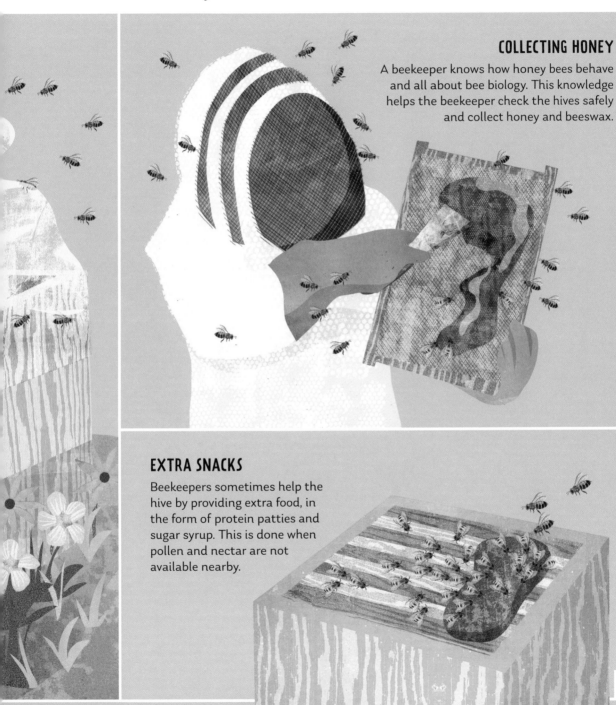

COLLECTING HONEY

A beekeeper knows how honey bees behave and all about bee biology. This knowledge helps the beekeeper check the hives safely and collect honey and beeswax.

EXTRA SNACKS

Beekeepers sometimes help the hive by providing extra food, in the form of protein patties and sugar syrup. This is done when pollen and nectar are not available nearby.

SAVE THE HONEY BEES!

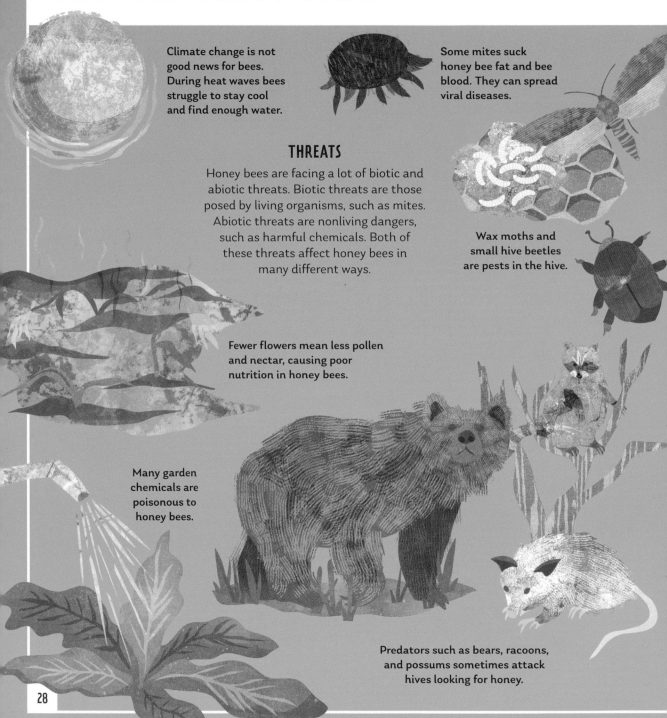

Climate change is not good news for bees. During heat waves bees struggle to stay cool and find enough water.

Some mites suck honey bee fat and bee blood. They can spread viral diseases.

THREATS

Honey bees are facing a lot of biotic and abiotic threats. Biotic threats are those posed by living organisms, such as mites. Abiotic threats are nonliving dangers, such as harmful chemicals. Both of these threats affect honey bees in many different ways.

Wax moths and small hive beetles are pests in the hive.

Fewer flowers mean less pollen and nectar, causing poor nutrition in honey bees.

Many garden chemicals are poisonous to honey bees.

Predators such as bears, racoons, and possums sometimes attack hives looking for honey.

There are many different factors that are posing a threat to honey bees all over the world. By identifying what is harming our honey bees, we can all do our part to help save them!

Plant bee-friendly flowering plants in your garden or in pots.

HOW CAN WE SAVE THEM?

There are many ways we can help honey bees. With the help of adults, we can make several changes in our gardens or on our balconies to protect the little critters.

Reduce your use of pesticides or become chemical-free to save honey bees.

Provide a variety of flowers that bloom throughout the different seasons.

Learn more about the honey bees and teach others. Support your local beekeeper!

Install bee hotels. Honey bees don't live in bee hotels, but they make great homes for other bee species.

Provide water for bees in hot summer months. Remember to add rocks or pebbles in these bee baths for the bees to stand on.

GLOSSARY

Beehive
An enclosed structure where a honey bee colony lives.

Beekeeper
A person who takes care of honey bees and collects honey from the hive.

Colony
A family of honey bees that lives inside a beehive.

Drone
A male honey bee.

Ecosystem
All living and nonliving things in an area. This includes animals and plants, as well as rocks and soil.

Honeycomb
A group of wax cells in the beehive.

Nectar
A sugary liquid that honey bees collect from flowers.

Pollen
A powdery substance that honey bees collect from flowers.

Predator
An animal that hunts, catches, kills, and eats other animals.

Proboscis
A honey bee's tongue. It acts like a straw to suck nectar and honey.

Queen bee
A female honey bee in a colony that can lay eggs. Each honey bee colony has just one queen.

Stinger
The sharp needlelike structure at the end of a worker honey bee's abdomen used for injecting venom.

Swarming
When a colony gets too big and the queen leaves with some workers to find a new nesting place.

Ultraviolet
Light rays produced by the sun that humans cannot see, but honey bees can!

Waggle dance
A special dance that worker honey bees use to tell other honey bees in the colony where food can be found.

Wax
A fatty substance that worker honey bees make to create honeycomb.

Worker bee
A female honey bee whose job is to maintain the hive. Most of the honey bees in a colony are worker bees.

Zoologist
A scientist who studies animals.

INDEX

This has been a

NEON SQUID

production

This book is dedicated to my parents, Pradip and Sutapa Chakrabarti, especially my father who always wanted me to write for children, and my husband Kashyap Basu, who is my rock and my pillar throughout. I also want to thank Dr. Ramesh Sagili for being a terrific mentor and an inspiration. And to all the young zoologists: be curious, try, fail, repeat, love, learn, and succeed!

Author: Dr. Priyadarshini Chakrabarti Basu
Illustrator: Astrid Weguelin

Editorial Assistant: Malu Rocha
US Editor: Allison Singer-Kushnir
Proofreader: Georgina Coles

Copyright © 2023
St. Martin's Press
120 Broadway, New York,
NY 10271

Created for St. Martin's Press
by Neon Squid
The Stables, 4 Crinan Street,
London, N1 9XW

EU representative: Macmillan
Publishers Ireland Ltd,
1st Floor, The Liffey Trust Centre,
117–126 Sheriff Street Upper,
Dublin 1, D01 YC43

10 9 8 7 6 5 4 3 2 1

The right of Dr. Priyadarshini Chakrabarti Basu to be identified as the author of this work has been asserted in accordance with the Copyright, Designs and Patents Act, 1988.

Library of Congress Cataloging-in-Publication Data is available.

Printed and bound by Vivar Printing in Malaysia.

ISBN: 978-1-684-49282-4

Published in January 2023.

www.neonsquidbooks.com